# ETHICAL
# DEBATES

## The Debate About
# Globalization

P9-DYP-715

## NATHANIEL HARRIS

rosen publishing's
**rosen
central**®

New York

Published in 2008 by The Rosen Publishing Group, Inc.
29 East 21st Street, New York, NY 10010

First Edition

Acknowledgments:
Individual case histories have been drawn from the following sources: Wu Zhaoxia from episode two, *Women of the Country*, of the BBC TV series *China*; Gilberto Ruiz Moreno from the website humanglobalization.org; Peter Chibize from "Zambia introduces free healthcare," an article by Shapi Shacinda; and Renson from the Fairtrade Foundation website.

Cover photograph: Downtown Bangalore—the third-largest city in India and a leading center of textile manufactures and foreign and domestic product distribution. The city is one of the stars of India's current phenomenal economic growth.
The author and publisher would like to thank the following for allowing their pictures to be reproduced in this publication: Archivio Iconografico SA/Corbis: 8. Remi Benali/Corbis: 38. Wesley Bocxe/Image Works/Topfoto: 40. Don Boroughs/Image Works/Topfoto: 14. Georgina Bowater/Corbis: 6. Geoff Caddick/ National Pictures/Topfoto: 37. Kevin Coombs/ Reuters/Corbis: 13. L. Demalteis/ Image Works/ Topfoto: 28. Macduff Everton/ Image Works/ Topfoto: 19. Monika Graff/Image Works/Topfoto: 30. M. Granitsas/Image Works/ Topfoto: 36.David Hartley/ Rex Features: 21. Yves Herman/Reuters/ Corbis: 22. Jon Hicks/ Corbis: 12. Fritz Hoffman/ Image Works/ Topfoto: 39. Keystone/Topfoto: 7. Jack Kutz/ Image Works/Topfoto: 43. John Maier/ Image Works/Topfoto: 1, 27. Gideon Mendel/ Corbis: 16. Miraflores/epa/Corbis; 15. Jeff Moore/ National Pictures/Topfoto: 44. Photri/ Topham: 25. Picturepoint/Topfoto: 9, 20, 41. Josef Polleross/Image Works/Topfoto: 45. Edy Purnomo/Image Works/Topfoto: 32. teve Raymer/Corbis: front cover, 35. Reuters/Corbis: 34. Ria Novosti/Topfoto: 24. Osvaldo Rivas/ Corbis: 26. Steven Rubin/Image Works/Topfoto: 4-5. Norbert Schiller/Image Works/Topfoto: 33. Sipa Press/Rex Features; 31. Sean Sprague/ Image Works/Topfoto: 18. Topham: 10.

Library of Congress Cataloging-in-Publication Data
Harris, Nathaniel, 1937-
    The debate about Globalization / Nathaniel Harris. -- 1st ed.
        p. cm. -- (Ethical debates)
    Includes index.
    ISBN-13: 978-1-4042-3753-7 (library binding)
    ISBN-10: 1-4042-3753-4 (library binding)
    1. Globalization--Juvenile literature. I. Title.
    JZ1318.H377 2007
    303.48'2--dc22
                                2006100798

Manufactured in China

# contents

# The Battle of Seattle

This real-life case study highlights some of the issues that surround the debate on globalization.

## case study

### "The Battle of Seattle"

It was the morning of November 30, 1999. The place was Seattle, the chief city of Washington State, on the western seaboard. Seattle was hosting a four-day meeting of the World Trade Organization (WTO), a powerful international body whose decisions affected every country. The delegates would soon leave their hotels and travel in a fleet of cars to the Paramount Theater for the opening ceremonies.

However, the protesters were on the move much earlier in the morning. By 7A.M. 1,000 were marching towards the center of Seattle, their numbers swelling rapidly. They carried large banners and puppet figures, and many of them wore red and yellow ponchos with anti-WTO slogans. Their first target was the Paramount Theater, which they surrounded, fully determined to let no one pass. Activists elsewhere locked arms and blocked road intersections to prevent delegates' cars from getting through. They had their first success when the opening ceremonies were canceled.

More and more protesters came to occupy central Seattle. Around noon, 20,000 U.S. trade unionists arrived, bringing the number present to at least 40,000. The majority of them were North Americans, but there

were also many who had made the long journey to Seattle from other continents. They represented hundreds of groups and organizations, from French and Philippine farmers to American steelworkers. All of them were opposed to WTO policies. Most believed the policies were deeply unfair and were harming the planet.

The scale of the protests took the Seattle police by surprise. Uncertain at first, they soon began to drive the crowds back with tear gas, concussion grenades, and pepper sprays; their violent behavior later led to the firing of the police chief. Most of the protesters made no attempt to fight back, although one small black-hooded group did try to smash up a Starbucks and some other stores, said to be big businesses favored by the WTO at the expense of poor people.

More typical were the protesters on the following day. They chanted "The world is watching," aware that the confrontations with the police were giving their cause worldwide publicity.

The disturbances continued, but the WTO did manage to meet—though, ironically, the nations represented failed to agree. It was now clear that there was wide hostility to the WTO and all it stood for. What it stood for is often described in a single word: globalization.

## summary

▶ This book deals with an issue—
globalization—that affects
everybody. It looks at conflicting
ideas about the present and future
state of the world, and at the values
on which those ideas are based.
There are no easy answers, and
readers will have to make up their
minds for themselves.

▼ "The Battle of Seattle": demonstrators wave
placards and banners to denounce the World
Trade Organization meeting in November
1999. They succeeded in disrupting some
events, and a violent police reaction ensured
worldwide publicity for the protesters' cause.

# CHAPTER 1.

# The global village

As early as 1962, a Canadian writer named Marshall McLuhan argued that the world was becoming a "global village"—a place where rapid, worldwide communications would make it possible to chat, make friends, do business, or shop as easily as people had always done in villages.

To an incredible extent the global village now exists, thanks to communications media such as the Internet, radio, television, and cellphones. Instant news and cheap, fast travel have made distant places seem near and familiar, so that people are deeply moved when a natural disaster strikes thousands of miles away. More routinely, fashions in clothes, entertainment, and even ideas catch on around the world in no time.

▼ The headquarters of Microsoft in Dubai: Microsoft has played a leading part in the communications revolution that has made the world a smaller place.

## Trade, finance, and globalization

Technological and other factors have worked to bring us closer to a single world society. This change has affected many areas of life, but has been most noticeable in the development of world trade. Goods, once normally produced in a single country, may now be made and assembled or processed in widely separate places, to

## It's a fact

In 1953 the total value of world trade was $80 billion. By 2004 it had multiplied a hundred times to reach $8 trillion. The most recent economic giant is China, with exports worth $762 billion and imports worth $660 billion. It has been widely predicted that China will become the world's largest economy by 2026 or even earlier.

▲ Shares being traded at the stock exchange in Frankfurt, Germany. Electronic links have made such places part of a global financial network.

be sold all over the world. Capital—the money or resources needed to start or expand enterprises—flows freely across national boundaries. Services such as banking or insurance are also available, often at the touch of a computer key, from stock exchanges and other financial markets. The markets, from New York and London to Hong Kong and Australia, are themselves increasingly linked and influenced by instant electronic information about global finance.

Globalization is the name given to the cluster of powerful processes that is binding the world together in this way. Globalization has created enormous wealth, but has also been accused of creating or making worse many of the world's great problems. It is said to have handed over the planet to powerful countries and big business, making poor countries even poorer. Uncontrolled

## viewpoints

"Globalization is political, technological, and cultural, as well as economic."
Anthony Giddens, *Runaway World*, 2002

"We cannot go back on globalization; it is here to stay. The issue is how we can make it work."
Joseph E. Stiglitz, *Globalization and Its Discontents*, 2002

globalization is blamed for damaging the environment, destroying local industries and traditions, and creating gigantic media empires that distort news and pour out bland, mindless entertainment.

These were some of the concerns given a high profile by the "Battle of Seattle" (see pages 4-5). The pro- and antiglobalization camps disagree violently about these issues, which do indeed raise many difficult practical and ethical questions.

## The history of globalization

Defenders of globalization like to point out that it is not a new process. In human history, ever since people spread out over the world, technologies, know-how, ideas, and goods have been passed backward and forward between communities. In the first century C.E., fashionable Roman women were wearing clothing made of silk that had been carried thousands of miles across Asia from China.

However, frequent and truly worldwide contacts began only a few hundred years ago. In the late fifteenth century, Europeans discovered the Americas and pioneered new sea routes that took them all around Africa to South Asia and the Far East. They became powerful, wealthy, and technologically advanced. They traded widely in, among other things, spices and slaves, and built up large colonial empires—lands on other continents that they ruled and sometimes settled with their own peoples.

## The Industrial Revolution

By the nineteenth century, Britain had become the leading trading nation and colonial power. Britain was the first country to experience a huge new leap forward—the Industrial Revolution—in which the harnessing of steam power heralded the age of factories, mass production, railroads, and a series of technological advances that have been virtually continuous ever since.

In the pre-industrial age, states had exercised considerable control over the economy, but in Britain businesses were increasingly left free to make their own decisions and compete with one another. It was generally believed that this "free market" would lead to the best results, including technological advances, maximum production, and low prices.

▼ The fifth-century Empress Theodora and her attendants at the East Roman court in Constantinople. The silk for their sumptuous robes was brought all the way across Asia from China.

▲ Mass production and machinery: the cutting room
of the Players tobacco factory in Britain around 1890.

The theory of this economic system, called capitalism, contradicted traditional ethics. It held that if individuals and businesses followed their self-interest rather than altruism (care for others), they would achieve the best possible economic outcome for everyone.

However, the Industrial Revolution meant that workers and their families were crowded into cities and factories, often in appalling conditions. The state found a new role in protecting people against abuses, for example by Factory Acts, which limited hours of work and the exploitation of women and children. The state also took over responsibility for areas such as education and public health, which had become of crucial importance in the new society.

## It's a fact

Rapid transportation draws the world together. The history of the modern railroad begins in Britain in 1829, when George Stephenson's famous "Rocket" locomotive won the Stockton-to-Darlington trials, achieving a speed of 30 miles (50 km) an hour. The first passenger line, between Liverpool and Manchester, opened in 1830. By 1900 there were 22,000 miles (36,000 km) of track in Britain alone, and trains could travel at 100 miles (160 km) an hour. By then, cars were already on the road, and three years later the Wright brothers made the first powered flights at Kitty Hawk, North Carolina.

## Free Trade and Protectionism

In buying from and selling to other countries, Britain championed Free Trade, which meant eliminating barriers to the free movement of goods between countries. The most important of these were tariffs—government taxes on imports (goods coming in from abroad). Britain abolished these, and most countries followed suit in the later nineteenth century. Other nations, such as the USA and Germany, emerged as Britain's competitors, and between about 1860 and 1914 world trade expanded at a breathtaking pace—faster, proportionately, than ever before or since.

World War I (1914-18) was a major upheaval that left the world in a far less stable condition. Most countries abandoned Free Trade, and an era of Protectionism began in which states protected their own industries at home by imposing tariffs on competing imports or giving the home industries financial help (known as subsidies). There were many crises during this period, including the Great Depression of the 1930s, when millions around the world were jobless.

## Switching economic policies

After World War II (1939-45), international institutions were set up to work toward renewed freedom of international trade. Considerable progress was made, and the most economically advanced nations, such as the USA, Canada, Germany, France, and Britain, enjoyed great prosperity. In most of these nations, the state had added to its functions, providing welfare payments for the unemployed, sick and old and, in some places, running socially important industries such as the water supply and the railroads.

▲ The Great Depression of the 1930s: unemployed workers line up outside an employment agency.

When this prosperity faltered, a powerful new trend emerged. Starting in the 1980s, beginning in the USA and Britain, there was a campaign to "roll back the state." Industries owned by the state were privatized (sold and turned into private companies), income taxes were lowered, and state spending was cut. Regulation and other restraints on businesses were abolished or weakened. In most wealthy societies, money (in such forms as finance, investment, and tourist spending) was allowed to move freely across countries. Thanks to the power of the USA and other economically advanced countries, this freeing of businesses operated internationally as well as nationally. It became easier to move goods, money, and factories from country to country. Reinforced by the "dot-com" revolution, which linked the world by computer, globalization roared ahead. It created a world society that was, to its admirers, incredibly dynamic, and, to its critics, tragically unstable and unjust.

## summary

▶ Globalization has been going on since very early times. It has generated great wealth, stacked the shelves of stores with goods from all over the planet, and brought the world's peoples closer together.

▶ On the other hand, the inequality and exploitation that have accompanied globalization have caused considerable suffering and continue to do so. This suggests to some critics that, at the least, it is being carried out in the wrong way, and that it should be controlled, slowed down, or even halted.

▼ Privatizations and other changes in the 1980s and 1990s often aroused violent opposition among people who feared they would suffer as a result. Here, demonstrators and riot police clash in Rio de Janeiro, Brazil, during a protest against the privatization of the state mining company.

## case study

### In the new China

In the 1980s, China changed its economic policy, opening up to the outside world. Rapid economic growth created gigantic changes. Teenager Wu Zhaoxia is one of millions of Chinese people who have left the poverty-stricken countryside for the cities. She lives and works in an electronics factory in Sanxiang. She puts in long hours and earns about $30 for a six-day week—but, as she told the BBC, her farmer parents "work from dawn to dusk" and are far worse off than she is. "I prefer it here." As well as the shopping and the nightlife, she enjoys a freedom that would have been impossible at home. Instead of an arranged local marriage, she has a boyfriend of her own choice, and she can pursue her dream of saving enough to set up a business of her own.

# CHAPTER 2

# Trade, wealth, and poverty

Globalization has affected how people live and think in all sorts of ways. The most obvious are economic—their standard of living, what jobs they do, and how secure they feel in them.

The previous chapter described the ideas that dominated the 1980s. They are often labeled neoliberalism: "neo" means new, and neoliberalism is seen as a revived version of the liberal or free market and free trade ideas of 1860-1914. In recent times, globalization has been driven by these neoliberal ideas, and many people think that globalization and neoliberalism are more or less the same thing. Neoliberals certainly claim credit for the achievements of globalization, notably the extraordinary prosperity of the USA, Canada, Western Europe, Japan, Australia, and several countries in southeast Asia.

Globalization and neoliberalism are not in fact the same. While some people may simply oppose globalization, others may favor it (in the form of an increasingly interconnected global society) but believe that neoliberal methods are misguided or need modifying. For example, these people may support globalization but think the poorest countries should be given economic help. It is natural to talk of being for or against globalization, but it is also important to keep these distinctions in mind.

▼ The glamorous, affluent face of the modern world: restaurants, cafés, and apartments in the prosperous southeast Asian city of Singapore.

▲ Gleneagles, 2005: a group photograph of the heads of the most powerful nations (the G8), the UN, the European Commission, and the World Bank, along with some other political leaders (see page 22 for more information about the Gleneagles summit).

## Running the world

Three international organizations, closely identified with neoliberalism, hugely influence the world economy. The first is the World Trade Organization (WTO), which was the target of the Seattle protesters (see pages 4-5). The WTO works to reduce tariffs and other barriers to the free movement of capital, goods, and services between countries. The second is the International Monetary Fund (IMF). Its function is to maintain stable rates of exchange between currencies. It is obviously easier for businesses and travelers to plan their operations if they know how much foreign currency they will get for their dollars, and that the rate is not likely to alter abruptly. The third international institution is the World Bank, which lends money to countries that have run into financial difficulties.

Most of the world's states are members of these organizations. However, in practice they are dominated by wealthy countries with advanced economies, led by the USA. Every year, the heads of these countries meet as "the G8" (Group of Eight) to make large policy decisions. The G8, seen as the source of the neoliberal policies promoted by the WTO and others, has also been targeted by antiglobalization protesters.

### It's a fact

The WTO has 149 members. As of June 2006, the latest negotiations to reduce tariffs and subsidies (the "Doha round," started in 2001) had failed to produce an agreement.
The IMF also has 149 members.
The World Bank consists of five organizations. The most important is the 180-member Bank for Reconstruction and Development.
The G8 members are the USA, Canada, the UK, France, Germany, Italy, Russia, and Japan.

**WHY PRIVATISE?**

Privatisation and Increased Investment is helping Uganda to become one of the fastest growing economies on earth.

Average Yearly Economic Growth Since 1990:
UGANDA = 6.6%
World Average = 1.8%

PRIVATISATION: A BETTER FUTURE FOR UGANDANS

▲ Propaganda for privatization in Uganda, Africa: many of its possible effects are discreetly passed over.

## A set of answers

The WTO holds meetings at which the member states negotiate over trade rules. The WTO and the World Bank also bring pressure on individual countries to run their economies along the neoliberal lines they favor. When a country asks the World Bank for a loan, it is likely to be told it can have the money—on condition that it "restructures" its economy.

Restructuring involves much more than bringing down tariff barriers. The country concerned is told it must cut taxes to encourage business activity. Cutting taxes reduces the state's income, but its government is also told to save money and balance its budget. The only way it can do this is by obeying the WTO's urging to privatize state-owned enterprises and spend less. Spending cuts very often hit social services such as education, healthcare, and payments to help the unemployed, the sick, and the old.

To neoliberals, restructuring is a valuable reform process and a necessary element in globalization. They regard a state that has to borrow as a state that has failed economically: it needs to change its ways, not just to borrow more and more.

## Undemocratic and unethical?

The counterarguments are ethical as well as practical. WTO-style policies are undemocratic. They are made by a body that is not elected and is not accountable to anybody for its decisions. They also impose radical changes on countries without giving their peoples any chance to approve or disapprove of them. The changes have often been deeply unpopular, causing riots and demonstrations such as those in Seattle.

A practical objection to the policies is that bodies such as the WTO impose their neoliberal remedies as though they fitted every case. Countries at different stages of development may have very different needs. A country that is dependent on selling a single crop abroad might reasonably want to spread the risks this poses to its economic well-being. It might try to start a new industry, protecting it with subsidies and tariffs until it is strong enough to compete with foreign concerns producing the same goods. But if it did so, the WTO would intervene, penalizing it for interfering with the free market. This happened to Mozambique, Ghana and other countries, which were forced to scrap such schemes.

## viewpoints

"The complaints against the WTO are hugely exaggerated, where not misconceived."
Martin Wolf, *Why Globalization Works*, 2004

"The problem is not that international trade is inherently opposed to the needs and interests of the poor, but that the rules that govern it are rigged in favor of the rich."
Amartya Sen, introduction to the 2002 Oxfam report *Rigged Rules and Double Standards*

▼ Politics and poverty: at a rally in the capital city of Caracas in 2004, the Venezuelan president Hugo Chavez denounces international financial institutions and the USA, which he and other Latin American radical leaders blame for their countries' troubles.

## The world's poor

Advocates of globalization have generally emphasized the long-term benefits of the process. Opponents counter that it has been a very long term, and that its end is nowhere in sight for the world's poor, who are often numerous even in countries hailed as successes for globalization. Many of them seem to have reaped little or no benefit from the process, despite the huge increase in world trade since the mid-twentieth century.

There are staggering differences in wealth between the world's more economically developed countries (MEDCs) and less economically developed countries (LEDCs). Many though not all less advanced countries are in Africa, where incomes are so low that a high proportion of the population are undernourished and always hungry. Disease is frequently rampant, many children die, and most people live shorter, unhealthier lives than they do in rich societies like the USA and UK. One large European country, Russia, became strikingly worse off when it abandoned its state-run economy and followed a neoliberal course in the early 1990s. Health, life expectancy, and

Sacks of American rice on sale in Port-au-Prince, the capital of Haiti, a desperately poor country in the Caribbean. In the 1990s Haiti lifted its trade barriers, enabling cheap imports such as U.S. rice to flood the market. This suited Haitians as consumers, but local farmers struggled to survive.

## viewpoints

"Never before have so many people—or so large a proportion of the world's population—enjoyed such large rises in their standards of living."
Martin Wolf, *Why Globalization Works*, 2004. Wolf's generalization is true because two populous countries, China and India, have experienced amazingly rapid growth in recent years; the statement gives no hint of the lack of progress made by most other LEDCs

"Is globalization only to benefit the powerful and the financiers, speculators, investors, and traders? Does it offer nothing to men, women, and children ravaged by the violence of poverty?"
Nelson Mandela, speaking at the 1999 Davos Economic Forum

employment levels plummeted dramatically for 15 years; only then did it seem possible that the country's valuable oil reserves might help its living standards to recover.

## Debt and interest

People in many poor states believe that globalization since the 1980s has worked to their disadvantage. Much statistical evidence suggests that these countries have become worse off over the past few decades, although the figures have been disputed. Many countries have certainly fared so badly that they are deep in debt—so deep that they can never get out.

When people borrow, they normally have to make regular payments as a return for using somebody else's money. These payments are known as interest. The larger the debt, the more interest has to be paid; and paying interest does not reduce the size of the debt. Some countries have debts so large that just paying the interest takes up a large proportion of the nation's income. They have no chance of paying off the debt itself, and after paying interest there is so little money left over that the country remains stuck in poverty.

case study

**A Mexican dairy**

Globalization reaches into remote places, and the process creates winners and losers. One of the winners is Gilberto Ruiz Moreno, a small-time dairy farmer in one of Mexico's poorest provinces, Chiapas. Gilberto started selling milk to a multinational food corporation that had set up in the area. Anxious to improve its yield and quantity, the corporation sent advisers to help Gilberto. Among the improvements they recommended was one that showed the benefits of globalization, since the advisers had learned it from Brazilian farmers. Cows were more productive when they were comfortable, and a simple sun-roof would protect them from the fierce Mexican sun. Although Gilberto was unconvinced at first, he was won over when the cows' yield increased and he tripled his sales.

This table shows average yearly income and life expectancy of people in some of the world's countries, 2004-5

| | Population (in millions) | GDP ($ billions) | Average yearly income per person ($) | Life expectancy |
|---|---|---|---|---|
| Burundi | 7.5 | 0.8 | 100 | 44 |
| Cambodia | 14.1 | 5.4 | 380 | 57 |
| Nicaragua | 5.5 | 4.9 | 910 | 70 |
| Bolivia | 9.2 | 9.3 | 1,010 | 65 |
| India | 1,094.6 | 785.5 | 720 | 63 |
| China | 1,034.5 | 2,228.9 | 1,740 | 71 |
| UK | 59.4 | 2,140.9 | 33,940 | 78 |
| USA | 293.5 | 11,667.5 | 41,400 | 77 |

GDP = Gross Domestic Product, the entire economic output of the country
Source: The World Bank

## Free and fair?

Free Trade theory claims that, where there are no trade barriers, competition between countries will lead them to specialize in the goods and services they can deliver most cheaply and efficiently. Efficient production and low prices will make it possible for every community to prosper.

In the real world things are not so straightforward, and it can be argued that Free Trade is not fair trade when it takes place between the powerful and the weak. MEDCs can control the terms of trade. Big corporations can fix prices to suit themselves, as has occurred in the case of many foodstuffs such as bananas and coffee. Poor countries cannot afford the investment, technology, and research they need to get new industries going. They are undersold and put out of business by competitors in advanced economies. Their only way out would be to use subsidies or tariffs to help the new enterprises until they could fend for themselves. A number of now advanced countries did this in the past when their economies were still weak, but now the World Trade Organization will not allow LEDCs to act in the same way.

It is argued therefore that even if LEDCs were not already in debt, they would find it impossible to compete with the West (a shorthand term often used to describe the economically advanced countries) and make significant progress. From their point of view, the WTO's version of globalization looks like a way of ensuring that the West maintains its economic mastery.

◀ A worker harvests coffee in the Central American republic of El Salvador. Coffee is the country's major cash crop, but prices on the world market fluctuate wildly. Producers here and in many other countries are able to earn, at best, a precarious living.

▲ A Mexican farmer gives corn to his neighbor to help with the crop yield. Cooperation helps poor farmers survive in a tough global environment. Many of their problems are caused by competition from cheap imports, or outside pressures that have made them turn to growing cash crops instead of food to feed themselves.

## Double standards

This view is supported by the West's double standards in relation to Free Trade. Major economic powers such as the USA and the European Union (EU) place tariffs on some imports and subsidize vulnerable sectors of their economies, for example agriculture, where LEDCs might otherwise compete effectively with their domestic produce. Though the subject is frequently aired, and promises are made, little gets done. The USA and six Central American states signed free trade agreements that came into force in 2006. At various points in the negotiations the U.S. representatives flatly refused any discussion of their agricultural protectionism.

## viewpoints

"The bottom line…is that liberal trade is beneficial. The obstacles to it, largely created by governments, need to be reduced."
Martin Wolf, *Why Globalization Works*, 2004

"The bigger and more powerful tend to succeed in 'free,' unregulated markets."
Will Hutton, *The World We're In*, 2002

Critics of this attitude are actually complaining that in such cases globalization, as the unhindered flow of finance, goods, and services, has not been thoroughgoing enough. Others interpret the situation as proving that globalization is not a "neutral" process, but one run by, and for the benefit of, the rich and powerful.

19

## Debt relief

Poverty and suffering in some deeply indebted countries are so great that western governments, as well as ordinary people and campaigners, have recognized something must be done about it. Western nations have long been giving aid to less economically developed countries, with only limited effect. It has often been misused, but it is also true that the amount of aid has been tiny when compared with interest and debt payments. A proposal that has attracted wide support is that some or all of these debts should be canceled. If this were done, borrower countries would no longer have debts they could not hope to repay. More important, they would not have to make crippling interest payments and could use the income saved to improve facilities such as roads, airports, healthcare, and education.

## A bad example?

Understandably, the idea of canceling debts was not welcomed by the creditor states and institutions. They argued it would set a bad example, encouraging debtors to stop paying what they owed or overspend. They also claimed in many instances the debtor states were to blame for their difficulties. Sometimes they simply mismanaged their affairs. There were also dictators who borrowed and then spent the funds on weapons or simply banked them for their own use. In other countries, corruption—theft and bribery—were rife. Often aid and loans were not used for the purposes intended, but were pocketed by officials or political big shots. On the other hand, the lenders knew who they were dealing with. A major reason for lending was often so that the borrower country could continue to buy the lender state's goods, which might well include arms that would keep a dictator or corrupt regime in power.

This debate raises some important ethical issues. What obligations do rich countries have to poor ones? Is it right for a country or an international institution to do business with an undemocratic regime? And if such a regime falls, is it right that the people it oppressed should inherit its debts, as they did, for example, when democracy was established in South Africa in 1994? The issue is not a simple one, since trade depends on contracts being honored. Serious consequences might follow if it was made too easy for a country to denounce its previous government and scrap all the agreements it had made.

## It's a fact

There are about 6 billion people in the world. In the early twenty-first century:1.3 billion lived on less than $1.38 a day and 2.8 billion lived on less than $2.55 a day. For every $1.96 in official aid that LEDCs received, they handed over $25 in debt repayments.
The 47 poorest countries owed $422 billion and paid $200 million in interest every week.

▼ Poverty in South Africa: a township just outside the national capital, Cape Town, in 2003.

## The fight against poverty

Although there was considerable resistance to the idea of debt relief, the West gradually accepted it. Even so, it was put into practice painfully slowly. In 1996 the Highly Indebted Poor Countries Initiative devised a program for 38 mostly African states (perhaps half of the world's very poor countries). It began to bring substantial results in 2005, following one of the most successful of all public campaigns, Make Poverty History.

The G8 summit at Gleneagles, in Scotland, announced substantial cuts in the debts owed by 18 countries and significant increases in aid.

Many felt that this was a substantial achievement, and that it was worth encouraging western governments to carry on down the same path. On the other hand, the deal involved a relatively small number of countries and did not in fact cover debts of every type. Moreover, debt relief was still accompanied by conditions

▼ Bono (left), lead singer of the U2 pop group, with José Manuel Barroso, president of the European Commission. Bono met the president on behalf of the Make Poverty History campaign. Celebrities like Bono have done much to publicize the plight of poor countries.

and could be seen as yet another way of imposing "liberalization" on those who received it. Nevertheless, governments and institutions had evidently accepted that the debtor nations had been unjustly treated. As so often, a more cynical view was possible—that debt-ridden countries are not good customers, and that relief measures would help keep the wheels of global trade turning.

Nevertheless, global poverty appeared to have found a place on the western agenda, firing the determination of ordinary people at least as much as their governments. It remained in question whether debt relief would end poverty without wider changes in the way world trade was carried on. This seemed confirmed when, within a year of the Gleneagles summit, organizations such as CAFOD (the Catholic Fund for Overseas Development) were expressing their disappointment at the exclusion of countries from WTO negotiations and the fierce WTO opposition to measures to protect the economies of LEDCs such as Zambia. There was evidently still no clear agreement on the way forward.

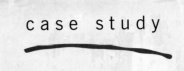

## case study

### Debt relief, pain relief

At the beginning of April 2006, 67-year-old Peter Chibize walked 12 miles (19km) from his village to a clinic in southern Zambia. He was suffering from a bad cough and pains in his chest and head. There was no way he could find the money it would cost him to be treated, but he felt so sick he went to the clinic anyway. When he was told treatment was now free, he was overjoyed and said "It was like a dream to me!" He took the good news, along with his painkillers, back to his village.

Peter probably never made the connection, but Zambia was able to provide free healthcare because part of the country's debts had been canceled following the 2005 G8 meeting (see page 22). However, there was still a problem: people were flocking to the clinics, but Zambia was desperately short of doctors and nurses. Evidently debt relief was part, but not all, of the solution to poverty in less economically developed countries.

## summary

- ▶ Defenders of neoliberal globalization say that institutions such as the World Trade Organization help countries in difficulties by giving them loans. Any conditions attached are for their own good.

- ▶ They also claim that unrestricted trade, tax cuts, and privatization bring prosperity to most people in the long run.

- ▶ Critics of globalization believe forcing such changes on countries is undemocratic and may only increase their economic disadvantage.

- ▶ They also point out that powerful countries press free trade on the poor and weak, while protecting their own industries. Where "free trade" involves commodities such as arms, it ought to be restrained.

# The politics of globalization

For several centuries, the nation state has been the most important form of political community. People identify themselves by their nationality, for example, as German or Japanese. They pay most of their taxes to their national government and, if necessary, serve in their national army.

Until recently, nation states were regarded as sovereign: that is they recognized no superior. They were free to organize their people's social and economic life as they thought best, to make alliances, and to wage war as and when they chose. However, in the last few years it has been claimed that national sovereignty has been weakened by international refusal to tolerate oppressive regimes, and that national freedom of action is being weakened by economic forces that cross national boundaries and bypass governments.

## UN involvement

International action is most associated with the United Nations (UN) and related international institutions, which are empowered to take action against states that wage aggressive wars or massacre their citizens. However, the members of the UN are themselves nation states, and energetic action tends to occur only when many states back it and are willing to provide the armed forces needed to intervene. The executive that runs the UN is far from being a world government and has no independent funding or forces of its own. As a result, by no means are all oppressive regimes targeted by UN action.

▼ A meeting of the United Nations (UN) General Assembly. The UN has not, as some hoped, developed into a world government.

▲ U.S. infantry in action during the American-led invasion of Iraq in 2003. The U.S. presence in the country suggested that traditional power politics were far from dead.

Nevertheless, in the 1990s and 2000s the UN was involved in crises in many parts of the world that would once have been regarded as remote. This did suggest that telecommunications changes (for example, instant, on-the-spot television news) had created a new global awareness among people in general. However, the UN seldom intervened effectively when the world's most powerful state, the USA, was unwilling to become involved. And in 2003, when the UN refused to give clear backing to an invasion of Iraq, directed against its dictator, Saddam Hussein, the USA and UK went ahead all the same. So it could be argued that little had really changed, and that the process of international politics was still ultimately based on national power, or lack of it.

There were other instances of globalization overriding national sovereignty. Among them were situations already described, in which debtor countries such as Ghana and Bolivia were forced by bodies like the WTO to alter ("restructure") some of their most important institutions. The governments of such countries did, of course, have the right to refuse and do without loans. But for really poor societies this sort of freedom of choice meant very little in practice.

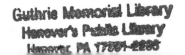

▲ Uncertain future: a textile factory in Managua, Nicaragua. In April 2006 Nicaragua ratified (consented to) the DR-CAFTA agreement, becoming part of a free trade area dominated by the USA.

## Regional groups

In recent times, a number of relatively wealthy countries have given up some of their political rights to work more closely with their neighbors. Large international trading blocs have been formed in several regions in order to remove trade barriers between members. Among these regional blocs are the 25-member EU (see page 19), the North American Free Trade Agreement (NAFTA), consisting of Canada, the USA, and Mexico, and the 10-member Association of Southeast Asian Nations (ASEAN). Their existence can be seen as a step toward complete globalization. On the other hand, regional trade blocs as often as not operate as protectionist groupings, and veto any trade-freeing agreement that might threaten the special economic interests of their members.

### It's a fact

NAFTA is the world's second-largest economic regional grouping, with a population of 400 million. Its members are Canada, the USA, and Mexico.
A new grouping, the Dominican Republic-Central America Free Trade Association (DR-CAFTA), came into force in 2006. It was envisaged as a stage in an eventual free trade area taking in all the Americas. The 25-member EU is currently the largest of the regional giants, stretching from the Irish Republic to Slovenia. It has a population of 455 million and accounts for over 40 percent of world exports (including trade between member states).

Currently the EU has the strongest common institutions and is often accused of becoming a "superstate"; its unpopularity in the early 2000s suggested that globalization had not yet seriously undermined national loyalties.

## Globalization and democracy

Globalization has often been praised on the grounds that it promotes democracy. Free-market economics encourage the growth of an educated middle class, which is said to be the necessary backbone of a stable democracy. The evidence of a direct link is not clear-cut, however, since many dictators have been enthusiastic free-marketeers.

## International giants

The most serious impact of globalization on state authority results from the growth of international big businesses. There are now many thousands of these corporations whose operations are not restricted to a single home country. Known as multinational or transnational corporations (TNCs), they invest, produce, and sell in a number of countries, and in some cases in more than one continent.

Multinationals dominate the world's trade, accounting for at least two-thirds of it. The biggest multinationals—corporations such as General Motors, Wal-Mart, and Exxon Mobil—are enormous and powerful. The annual sales of one of these giants are greater than the entire economic output (GDP or Gross Domestic Product) of many countries, and not just the poorest. In fact, 51 out of the 100 leading world economies are multinationals—only 49 are states.

▼ Global giant: a Walmart supermarket in São Paulo, Brazil—one store in the multinational's worldwide empire.

"We are seeing sovereignty shift into corporate hands. Power is passing from governments to TNCs [transnational corporations or multinationals] and the poor are paying the highest price."
John Madeley, *Big Business, Poor Peoples*, 1999

"When one looks closely one finds that corporations are not more powerful than countries and do not dominate the world through their brands."
Martin Wolf, *Why Globalization Works*, 2004

## The impact of the multinationals

It is not surprising that these giant corporations have a strong influence on political affairs. Governments of poor countries are in a weak position when they negotiate with multinationals. They are anxious for multinationals to set up subsidiaries (branches, technically separate from the parent company) in their countries, bringing in money and goods

▼ A Mexican man makes trousers for export to the USA. He is paid about $5 a day, though the garments will sell for much more. Is he being exploited—or lucky to earn so much?

and providing employment for local people. This enthusiasm is strong evidence that the activities of multinationals bring real benefits to developing countries.

However, the benefits may be restricted to the governing or wealthier classes, or to a relatively small number of employees, while the mass of the people suffer as a result of the concessions made to the multinationals. Given a free hand, multinationals may behave in ways that damage some communities, for example taking over tribal lands and driving away their peoples, using up local resources such as water, or polluting the environment.

Multinationals certainly tend to react angrily to attempts to improve working conditions or apply health-and-safety standards in their concerns. They have often been accused of flouting the laws of host nations while their governments, anxious to keep the multinationals in the country, look the other way. Multinationals have also been accused of preferring to operate in states with dictatorial regimes, where popular protests, trade unions, and other forms of opposition are not tolerated. In dictatorships, and in some democracies, the government may step in to stifle protests against the activities of the multinationals.

## The profit motive

When multinationals act in such ways, it is because they are essentially profit-seeking organizations. Their reason for existence is to make money for their owners, the corporation's shareholders. Many who favor globalization would say that companies can function efficiently only in that way. However, it can also be argued that benevolent and ethical behavior is an obligation that applies to all, organizations as well as individuals. In 2006, when the British parliament considered a Company Law Reform Bill, attempts were made to put a "Duty of Care" clause into it. This would have obliged company directors to take seriously the effects of their plans on communities and the environment. The attempt failed, perhaps because even the politicians of wealthy countries are reluctant to offend powerful corporations. In practice, multinationals are often more vulnerable to bad publicity, when newspapers or television programs investigate their behavior and reveal facts that may cause customers to turn away from them, reducing their profits.

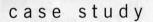

## case study

### Tragedy in Nigeria

Ken Saro-Wiwa was one of Nigeria's best-known writers. In 1990 he founded the Movement for the Survival of the Ogoni People. The Ogoni live in part of the Niger Delta, where Shell and other oil companies were operating. Saro-Wiwa claimed that the companies were taking over Ogoni lands and polluting the atmosphere, soil, and water to a catastrophic extent. Nigeria's military government was actively involved, and, the UK was supplying the government with the arms it required to suppress discontent. In 1993, after demonstrations by 300,000 people, Shell suspended its operations. The military dictatorship responded by killing a number of activists and arresting Saro-Wiwa and eight other Ogonis. Their unfair trial sparked international protests, but they were all executed in November 1995. Oil extraction in the Niger Delta remains a controversial issue.

▲ A demonstration against sweatshops (workplaces where conditions are bad and wages low), held during a meeting of the World Economic Forum in February 2001. The grotesque heads represent big-business leaders.

## The power of multinationals

All states find it hard to control an organization with many branches that are beyond its frontiers and not subject to its laws. If the multinational is a major investor and employer, the possibility that it will withdraw its operations and relocate to a different country is likely to alarm almost any government. For this reason, governments may easily be persuaded to lower the rate of taxation on the multinational's profits or relax labor laws to make it easier for the multinational to control its workforce. Another way of interpreting this situation is to see western governments and multinationals as allies, working toward the same goals in the globalization project. For all their supposed lack of nationality, the great majority of multinationals have their headquarters in the most economically powerful countries (especially the USA, Germany, and Japan) and retain something of a national character.

Workers in the West tend to be suspicious of multinationals. As well as pressing for relaxations of labour laws, multinationals will readily switch their operations from one country to another, leaving job losses once they have gone. Even nationally based firms are not above outsourcing—

relocating some operations to a country where labor costs are cheaper. However, the result is usually to bring employment to a poorer country, so it seems inconsistent to bemoan poverty in the developing world and blame multinationals for western job losses. Arguably one of the roles of the supposedly weakened state should be to take actions that soften the impact of job losses on communities.

## Globalization and the state

Another alleged result of globalization is that states are losing control over their own destinies. Capital, goods, services, and technologies now flow, uncontrolled and in huge quantities, across frontiers, locating and relocating in different parts of the world. These are said to limit the state's control of economic activity within its borders or even to prevent it from setting the value of its own currency. Economic forces and events elsewhere in the world, it is argued, have a greater impact than decisions made by a national government.

Employees at a call center ► in New Delhi, India; because English is widely spoken in India, call centers have been set up there for British telephone services. In the UK this "outsourcing" has led to protests from workers fearful of losing their jobs.

## Are states becoming feebler?

Enthusiasts for neoliberal globalization usually approve of the weakening of state power, believing that markets are wiser than governments. Those who disagree point out that most states, even in the nineteenth century (regarded as the free-market "golden age"), have tried to protect their societies from undesirable aspects of economic activity, for example by passing laws to regulate working conditions and limit industrial pollution. They point to many failures and abuses associated with uncontrolled market forces, from stock market crashes to environmental damage. In recent times, the rapid electronic movement of money from country to country has added to the risks, especially where the money is used to make quick profits rather than for long-term investment. A sudden flood and an equally sudden withdrawal of funds can have a destabilizing effect on a country's economy and threaten wider consequences. In recent times, serious monetary crises have affected Mexico (1994), Southeast Asia (1997), and Argentina (2001).

Whether states are really powerless in the face of general trends is hotly debated. Some observers think that governments could do a good deal, separately and together, if they really wanted to. They certainly act vigorously where their vital interests are concerned. For example, according to freemarket theories, labor should travel unhindered from place to place, responding to market forces. In practice, countries police their borders and restrict immigration, deciding which type of applicant will suit them.

▼ The price of failure: thousands of scavengers on an Indonesian dump look for anything they can use or sell. After a national economic crisis in 1997, the numbers on the site increased dramatically. Indonesia is still deeply in debt.

▲ In poverty stricken, war-scarred Somalia, militias have ample foreign-made weaponry.

Governments also outlaw and try to exclude substances they consider harmful to their society, particularly drugs. Their activity can be contrasted with the behavior of multinationals that sell unhealthy products, such as cigarettes, in poor countries. Western governments are often active in assisting arms manufacturers in their countries to sell weapons abroad, fueling wars and civil wars. Such operations raise obvious ethical issues concerning the conflict between profit, or national self-interest, and a wider duty to humanity.

One view of current politics is that it could benefit from globalization, since only a world government could successfully regulate the operations of multinationals and financiers. The G8 is often described as "the unofficial world government," and its own website recognizes its "centrality in the process of world governance." However, the G8 and its most powerful member, the USA, are deeply committed to neoliberalism and are unlikely to move toward stricter control of globalization.

## summary

▶ Globalization, some people have argued, weakens governments, which too often hamper the operation of free markets.

▶ Multinational corporations bring jobs to LEDCs where labor is cheap, and then move on when this brings prosperity and increased costs; and so more and more countries raise their living standards.

▶ Multinationals seek profit wherever it can be found and therefore, critics say, may behave unscrupulously unless controlled.

▶ Arguably governments could do more to control multinationals, and international authority should also be increased.

# CHAPTER 4

# Planetary matters

Globalization is a process with huge economic and political consequences. It also has a wider impact on human life and the health of the planet.

Globalization has intensified the production and rapid distribution of relatively cheap, mass-produced goods, such as packaged or fast foods, T-shirts and running shoes, DVDs and MP3s, motorbikes and cars. These are part of the affluent lifestyle of advanced economies. They are often made, but not widely used, in less advanced countries, and one view is that they ought to be available to many more of the world's peoples. However, there are concerns about the way in which such goods invade and dominate world markets. Some commentators believe that this is forging a single world culture, reinforced by media which create a global vogue for pop music, fashions, and sports. All of these are typical of western, mainly American, culture which is said to be swamping all other ways of life.

## "Cookie cutter culture"?

People who oppose this trend voice a number of objections to it. Processed and branded produce in supermarkets, and fast food and soft drinks in restaurants, are often attacked for being nutritionally poor and promoting obesity. Goods that are cheap and marketed by powerful corporations destroy the demand for locally produced quality goods. Above all, globalization is accused of creating a single,

▼ At a McDonald's restaurant in Jakarta, the Indonesian capital, staff wear Islamic clothing, apparently to avoid accusations that McDonald's is hostile to Islam, or a westernizing influence.

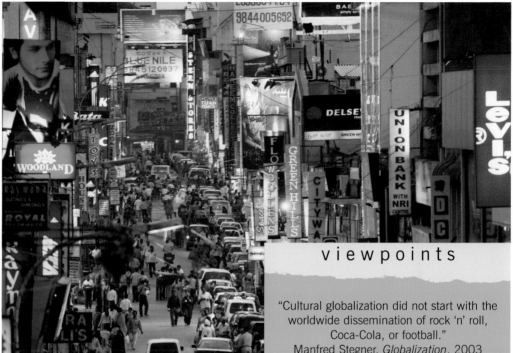

"Cultural globalization did not start with the worldwide dissemination of rock 'n' roll, Coca-Cola, or football."
Manfred Stegner, *Globalization*, 2003

▲ Downtown Bangalore in southern India, crowded with people and cars and flooded with brightly lit advertisements. Bangalore has become the third-largest city in India, following a rapid expansion that made it a leading center of textile manufacturing and foreign and domestic product distribution. The city is one of the stars of India's current phenomenal economic growth. However, this has been achieved at a cost, widening the gap between rich and poor, hurting some groups, and raising serious environmental issues.

"There should be more places like this one [a big new shopping mall] in Beijing. They have everything you could want, and even things you never realized that you wanted."
A young Chinese woman interviewed by the BBC

bland, worldwide "Cookie cutter culture" in which the same styles in food and clothes, ideas and buzz-words, sports, music, and television will prevail.

Globalization has certainly had a great impact on ancient and once remote peoples and cultures; but opposition to it also comes from advanced countries. For example, a good many people in France dislike what they see as the Americanization of their country. They are proud of their distinctive national traditions and oppose the "invasion" of English words into the French language as well as U.S.-style fast food chains and Hollywood movies. The French state has come to the aid of the national movie industry, restricting the number of non-French movies shown and giving financial help to the home industry. One of the best known figures in the antiglobalization movement is a French farmer, José Bové, who first came to notice by attacking a McDonald's building.

## Quality of life

Debates on subjects such as quality of life and diversity sound rather wooly but are deeply felt. Many people treasure human and environmental diversity, though they might have difficulty in making a clear-cut case for it in ethical, let alone material, terms. On the other side it can be argued that, in the modern world, people are free to make choices, good or bad, and that they clearly choose the prevailing global culture. If French people did not want to watch American movies, there would be no call for regulations to limit the number imported. Moreover, even in France local decisions have not always been opposed to

"Cookie cutter culture," for example, when a local French authority welcomed the siting of Euro Disney in its area.

In practice, defenders of globalization also appear to value diversity, and claim that the process does not really harm it. They argue that when mass-produced goods and services meet everyday needs, other kinds of goods and services do not disappear, but become specialties that increasingly affluent customers can afford to buy when they need them. The availability of ready-to-wear suits does not prevent buyers from patronizing tailors who make clothes to measure. Some crafts or cultures may disappear, but new ones take their place. As in the past, change is inevitable.

## Infotainment and dumbing down

Similar arguments rage over media such as television and movies. According to one view, these are effectively propaganda for western values. Their products are made for a mass audience, and have too much money invested in them for the makers to risk any kind of original or unorthodox approach. As usual, there are conflicts of opinion about the accuracy of this picture. Are news programs being turned into "infotainment," jazzed up to keep the interest of supposedly inattentive viewers? Are programs in general being "dumbed down"?

A closely related issue is the power of advertising. Some commentators scoff at

◀ The CNN newsroom in Atlanta, Georgia: CNN (Cable News Network) was founded in 1980 by Ted Turner, who introduced the idea of 24-hour news coverage. CNN International is said to be watched in more than 200 countries, making it a striking example of the global reach of modern media. There are, however, widely different views as to whether the media operate to shape, or simply reflect, people's tastes and opinions.

the idea that advertising can brainwash people into liking or wanting things unless they find that they do like or want them. On the other hand, advertising saturates people with images that are surely bound to influence them. The message of commercial advertising is that the good life is about buying and consuming more and more things. There is no end to it, since consumption must go on forever if corporations and economies are to thrive.

## It's a fact

In 2004, more than 90 percent of the U.S. media market was owned by six corporations, which also had wide international holdings. They were:
General Electric (revenue $65.5 billion)
Time Warner ($42.1 billion)
Walt Disney ($30.8 billion)
Bertelsmann ($23.2 billion)
Viacom ($22.5 billion)
Newscorp. ($20.4 billion)

## case study

### "The McLibel Two"

In 1990 two London environmental activists, Helen Steel and Dave Morris, were handing out pamphlets that condemned the fast-food company McDonald's for the poor nutritional quality of its products, its treatment of employees, misleading advertising targeting children, and other shortcomings. Threatened by the company, Steel and Morris refused to back down, and McDonald's began a legal action against them for libel (writing maliciously about someone). Steel and Morris argued the case themselves against top lawyers hired by McDonald's. It lasted a record two-and-a-half years, generating hugely unfavorable publicity for the company as the "McLibel Two" proved that a number of their charges were true. McDonald's won a technical victory, later (2005) canceled by the European Court of Human Rights. Fast food, especially when served in schools, became an important public issue.

◀ Helen Steel and Dave Morris outside a McDonald's in central London, on February 15, 2005. They were celebrating the end of a 15-year struggle. The European Court of Human Rights had just overturned their conviction for libel, citing the unfairness of Britain's libel laws.

▲ Workers laying the Baku-Supsa oil pipeline, running from Azerbaijan to Turkey. It went into operation in 1999, transporting 100,000 barrels of oil a day. Since the 1990s, new pipeline building has boomed, maintaining supplies regarded as essential to the world economy, but raising environmental and security concerns.

## Globalization and the environment

If globalization means ever-increasing consumption, the consequences for the planet could be grave. Some corporations are regularly accused of being agents of pollution. Even more serious charges are that the forces of globalization are exhausting the planet's natural resources and destroying its health.

These are complex, wide-ranging issues, which can only be outlined in this book. A belief that globalization will exhaust many natural resources is based on the rate at which commodities such as oil and minerals are being extracted, and the obvious fact that they exist only in finite (limited and impossible-to-increase) amounts. The most discussed of these resources is oil, which drives the entire world economy and also provides people in the West with personal benefits (such as cars and cheap air travel) are widely regarded as impossible to do without.

## Conflict of views

Corporations invest huge sums in searching for untapped oil reserves, and hopes of finding alternative energy sources are frequently expressed. Nevertheless, advocates of Free Trade claim that alarms over the exhaustion of resources are exaggerated. They point out that some predictions of doom have already been disproved. They believe that human ingenuity and inventiveness have been underestimated, and that profit-seekers will find technological solutions to the problems as the rewards for doing so become ever greater. An alternative view is that doing nothing is convenient for the West, allowing it to carry on with its heavy-consumption lifestyle. If so, the world may have to pay dearly in the long run.

There are many other environmental concerns linked to globalization, from the clearing of the Amazonian rain forest to the building of gigantic dams. The global

steamroller is also having a disastrous effect on plant and animal species, which are becoming extinct in unprecedented numbers. This again raises the issue of diversity: just how much value do we place on natural diversity and, in practical terms, what benefits are we prepared to sacrifice in order to preserve it?

## v i e w p o i n t s

"Entirely new approaches are needed to redirect society toward goals of equilibrium rather than growth."
Club of Rome report, 1970

"After all, almost everyone believes in growth."
Joseph E. Stiglitz, *Globalization and Its Discontents*, 2002

▼ China's Three Gorges Dam under construction; it controversially led to the displacement of huge numbers of people.

▲ New Orleans flooded, 2005: climate change may
have been at least partly responsible.

## The big issue?

If the majority of scientists are correct,
global warming is the greatest
environmental issue of the twenty-first
century. Much of the warming is a result
of the greenhouse gases present in the
atmosphere, which trap the sun's heat.
As a consequence, global temperatures are
certain to increase, causing rising sea levels
and other environmental changes, along
with increasingly extreme weather
patterns. A major source of greenhouse
gases is the burning of fossil fuels such as
oil, gas, and coal—the very energy sources
that drive the global economy.

The problem is so serious that the nations
of the world have come together and tried
to agree on a program of action. Some
progress has been made, but there are
great obstacles. One is the reluctance of
rich nations to change a way of life based
on central heating, air conditioning, heavy
car use, and cheap flights. The richest
country of all, the USA, was slow to accept
the reality of global warming and refused to
sign up to an international agreement, the
1997 Kyoto Protocol, committing countries
to cutting greenhouse gas emissions.

## The future at stake

Another obstacle is the understandable
wish of non-western states to make
substantial economic progress, although
that would inevitably mean increased
production of greenhouse gases. This
has already happened in India and China,
where breakneck economic growth has
been accompanied by very high energy
use and environmental damage. Such

states might well argue that it is their turn to achieve affluence, and that it is time for the West to make any sacrifices needed to save the planet. This kind of standoff will probably be avoided, but it does highlight yet another problem at the heart of globalization. If its advocates are right, and never-ending growth does eventually spread wealth in all directions and bring worldwide prosperity, the planet will almost certainly be unable to sustain the resulting level of consumption.

This would appear to be true even if technological solutions were found to the dwindling of natural resources and the impact of global warming. Some people may argue that the prospect of global affluence is a pleasant but remote prospect, best tackled if and when it happens. By contrast, many individuals

and groups in the antiglobalization movement put sustainable development among the new strategies they propose.

## summary

▶ According to some critics, globalization is creating a uniform world. The media are controlled by an increasingly small number of corporations which stifle originality and brainwash audiences.

▶ The global economy depends on ever-increasing consumption which, it has been predicted, the planet will be unable to sustain.

▶ A counterargument is that globalization offers people a wider range of choices, enabling them to express their individuality as never before.

▶ Although planetary problems need to be tackled, the way forward is arguably through technological progress, not retreat.

▼ People struggle for breath in the smog in China, where the "economic miracle" has involved severe pollution.

# CHAPTER 5

# Globalization and its opponents

The "Battle of Seattle" (see pages 4-5) was not the first protest against globalization, but it was the first to make an international impact. Since then, mass demonstrations or "alternative" gatherings have accompanied meetings of the major institutions concerned with the world economy, and some have erupted into serious violence. Ironically, globalization has made it possible for protesters to organize effectively. Instruments of global communication such as the Internet and cellphones now enable people from many countries to confer, make plans, and coordinate their actions.

Representatives of the international institutions began by loftily declaring that the protesters were misguided and ignorant. However, the strength of their feelings was unmistakable and it was hard not to be impressed by a cause that brought together American trade unionists, villagers from the Andes, French farmers, women's groups protesting against discrimination, Indian miners, and many others. Politicians like U.S. President Bill Clinton were quicker to react than the unelected WTO, but eventually the institutions did admit that mistakes had been made, although significant changes in their behavior were slow in coming.

### The many faces of protest

The protesters come from a variety of backgrounds and do not necessarily have identical beliefs and aims. Some may be

more concerned with their own grievances and special interests than the state of the world. A number are nationalists, angry at the way globalization interferes with their countries' affairs. Some are socialists, who believe the state should own important industries and control the economy for the common good. Yet others are anarchists, violent or nonviolent, who want to replace governments with cooperative communities that run their own affairs; one small anarchist group was generally held responsible for some store-wrecking, which occurred during the Seattle protests.

However, the majority of protesters are people who oppose neoliberal globalization because of its failure to relieve poverty and its negative impact on the environment. They probably share a vision of a more cooperative, more locally and democratically run world, not hostile to trade but also not dominated by profit-driven economies and corporations. Whether such a vision is practical is very much a matter of opinion.

The objectives of the majority of protesters are most clearly expressed by the campaigning organizations that work to combat some of the undesirable consequences of globalization. Friends of the Earth, ActionAid, Oxfam, Christian Aid, Greenpeace, and many others have an international reach. They are described as nongovernmental organizations (NGOs). Some began as charities, working to end poverty, while others were dedicated to saving the environment. These differences still appear in the way they angle their campaigns but, significantly, both types of NGO have increasingly come to focus on the issue of globalization.

▼ Activists at a protest against the World Trade Organization's policies, timed to coincide with the WTO meeting at Cancun, Mexico, in September 2003. Demonstrators were kept 6 miles (10 km) away from the convention center, but still made a significant impact.

## case study

### The banana farmer

Renson is a banana farmer from El Guabo in Ecuador. He had to leave school early to help his parents on their banana farm. Now an adult, he belongs to the El Guabo cooperative, a group of farmers who help one another. They deal directly with Fairtrade, which means that Renson receives a good price for his bananas, unaffected by the ups and downs of the world market. Encouraged by Fairtrade, he stopped using chemicals on his land, and he thinks his bananas taste better as a result. More secure than in the past, Renson has been able to build a new house, and he hopes to give his two children a better education than he had.

## Campaigning for change

The NGOs have raised public awareness of the globalization issue in the West, and campaigns such as Make Poverty History seem to have had a real influence on political and economic decision-makers. There has also been considerable public support for more ethical, less profit-driven economic activity. In 1997, the British government announced that it would follow an "ethical foreign policy," though its subsequent involvement in arms dealing tarnished that initiative. Individuals and some firms committed themselves to "ethical investment," refusing to put money into, or do business with, enterprises that exploited poor countries or damaged the environment. Some multinationals signed up to follow codes of conduct that were, in effect, promises to behave ethically.

▼ The British prime minister, Tony Blair, and his wife on the steps of their official residence, 10 Downing Street, in London. They are receiving some of the 2.5 million letters written supporting the Make Poverty History campaign.

◀ A worker at El Guabo Banana Cooperative in the village of Libertad, Ecuador. Cooperatives are based on mutual aid and a pooling of resources that improves the individual farmer's chance of surviving. Opinions differ as to whether they, or initiatives such as Fairtrade, can change the larger economic picture.

## Ethical brands

Another development was the growing market for "Fairtrade" products, purchased at prices that assured producers of a living wage and some money over to invest in improvements. Fairtrade goods cost a little more, but many people were happy to pay the extra. These and similar initiatives indicated a real urge to put the world to rights. However, skeptics pointed out that the sacrifices involved were small, and that meanwhile westerners were buying more gas-guzzling cars and in general enjoying a standard of living that ultimately rested on the inequalities they denounced. As with almost every aspect of globalization, what needed to be done and what was likely to be done remained very much in question.

## summary

▶ A positive view of globalization is that, like every human project, it may need some adjustment, but that scrapping it would bring terrible, destructive results.

▶ The worldwide movement against globalization is itself made possible by globalization. Reconciling ethics with politics is an old problem, not one created by globalization.

▶ A radically different view is that the only hope for the human future is a world based on sustainable economics and ethical standards.

# Glossary

**Anarchist** A person who believes that governments and other authorities should be replaced by cooperative communities that run their own affairs. There are violent and nonviolent forms of anarchism.

**Bribery** Unlawful payment, made to an official or other person in authority, in return for favorable treatment, for example, the award of a government contract.

**Colonial** Describes a colony (see below) or the system of having colonies.

**Colony** A territory that belongs to a state; until recently, European states had many colonies in other continents.

**Democracy** A system of government in which rulers are elected by the people. Countries and organizations may be democratic or undemocratic, depending on whether the majority is represented in them.

**Dictator** A ruler who holds absolute power.

**Free market** A situation in which there are no artificial barriers to prevent businesses competing on level terms and consumers making free choices.

**Free Trade** Trade between countries unhampered by state-imposed tariffs or subsidies.

**G8** The Group of Eight, an organization consisting of eight of the world's most economically advanced countries.

**International Monetary Fund (IMF)** An international organization set up to maintain stable rates of exchange between currencies.

**Multinational corporations** Big businesses whose operations give them a stake in a number of countries. They are more correctly, but less commonly, known as transnational corporations.

**Nation state** A state whose inhabitants feel themselves to be a single people.

**Neoliberalism** Economic doctrine that emphasizes the free market (see above) and tends to be hostile to all forms of state ownership, control, or regulation of business activity.

**Propaganda** Statements and ideas that are distorted or put over in a biased way in order to influence people.

**Protection** The use of tariffs and subsidies to protect a country or group's industries from outside competition. As a policy, it is known as Protectionism.

**Subsidy** Financial help given to an industry, most often by the state and in order to help the industry fight off foreign competition.

**Tariffs** Taxes on imported goods. As well as enriching the state, tariffs make imports more expensive and so help the sales of untaxed (and therefore relatively cheap) home-produced goods.

**Trade bloc** A group of states that follow an agreed set of rules in their dealings with one another and states outside the bloc.

**Trade union** An organization of workers, formed to defend or improve pay and conditions.

**Undemocratic** The opposite of democratic, (see above).

**United Nations (UN)** An organization of which all the world's states are members. It was founded in 1945 in the hope of solving disputes peacefully.

**West, the** The world's economically advanced countries. These are no longer all in North America or Western Europe, but the term continues to be used.

**World Trade Organization (WTO)** An international organization that works to remove tariffs and other barriers to the free movement of capital, goods, and services between countries.

**World Bank** An international bank; it lends money to states that have run into difficulties.

# Timeline

**1492** Christopher Columbus reaches the Americas.

**1497-8** Vasco da Gama pioneers a sea route from Europe to the East.

**1522** Ferdinand Magellan's ship *Victoria* is the first vessel to sail around the world.

**1760** Beginnings of the Industrial Revolution in Britain.

**1860** Free Trade era begins. Great prosperity in Western Europe and North America.

**1914-18** World War I. Beginning of a new protectionist era. Shrinking of world trade.

**1929** Wall Street (the U.S. stock exchange) crashes. The Great Depression of the 1930s follows the Wall Street Crash.

**1939-45** World War II.

**1970s** Many less economically developed countries become deeply indebted.

**1980s** Neoliberalism becomes the dominant economic doctrine. Globalization speeds up.

**1991** Russia begins a disastrous changeover from state-controlled to freemarket economy.

**1994** Mexican monetary crisis.

**1995** Nigeria: execution of Ken Saro-Wiwa and other Ogoni activists.

**1996** Highly Indebted Poor Countries Initiative.

**1997** Monetary crisis in Malaysia and other Southeast Asian states.

**1999** The "Battle of Seattle."

**2001** Monetary crisis in Argentina.

**2005** Make Poverty History campaign. G8 leaders promise debt relief for 18 countries.

# Further information

Books to read:

***The Globalisation Issue***
Craig Donnellan
(Independence, 2005)

***Global Warming***
Susannah Bradley
(Aladdin/Watts, 2005)

***Planet Under Pressure: Energy***
Clive Gifford
(Raintree, 2006)

***Protecting Species and Habitats***
Sue Barraclough
(Watts, 2006)

**Due to the changing nature of Internet links, The Rosen Publishing Group, Inc., has developed an online list of Web sites related to the subject of this book. This site is updated regularly. Please use this link to access the list:**
**www.rosenlinks.com/ed/global/**

# Index